D0777128

Seeds of a Nation

Illinois

Books in the Seeds of a Nation series include:

Seeds of a Nation

ILLINOIS

Illinois

P. M. Boekhoff and Stuart A. Kallen

KidHaven Press

KidHaven Press, an imprint of Gale Group, Inc.
P.O. Box 289009, San Diego, CA 92198-9009

On cover: *LaSalle and Party Arrive at the Village of the Illinois. January 1, 1680,* by George Catlin

Library of Congress Cataloging-in-Publication Data

Boekhoff, P. M. (Patti Marlene), 1957–
    Illinois/by P. M. Boekhoff and Stuart A. Kallen.
        p. cm. — (Seeds of a nation)
    Includes bibliographical references and index.
    Summary: Discusses the early Native Americans in Illinois, French settlers, the fur trade, battles between Native American tribes and Europeans, and statehood.
    ISBN 0-7377-0279-6 (hardcover: alk. paper)
    1. Illinois—Juvenile literature. [1. Illinois.] I. Kallen, Stuart A., 1955– . II. Title. III. Seeds of a nation (Series)
    F541.3 .B64 2002
    977.3—dc21

00-012811

Printed in the U.S.A.

Contents

The Original People

Illinois is a leading urban, manufacturing, and agricultural state in the Midwest region of the United States. It is bordered on the north by Wisconsin, on the northeast by Lake Michigan, on the east by Indiana, on the west by Iowa and Missouri, and on the south by Kentucky. Although Illinois is the twenty-fourth largest state in size, it has the sixth largest population of all states, with over 12.1 million people living there in 2000.

Earth Islands in a Sea of Corn

Today Illinois is inhabited by people from all over the world, but until the seventeenth century, only Native American people lived in the region. Between A.D. 500 and 1500, southwestern Illinois was the center of one of the greatest Native American civilizations in North

America. The original people, called the Mississippians, built major cities atop more than ten thousand earth mounds along the banks of the Mississippi River east of present-day St. Louis.

The ancient earth mounds were shaped like flat-topped pyramids and surrounded by cornfields. The natives called these mounds "earth islands" because in midsummer they rose above a sea of ripening corn that stretched as far as the eye could see. This corn fed a large population of people and made it possible for them to build a long-lasting civilization.

As the population of the area grew, the Mississippians developed a central government and system of trade. They created a network of walking trails and river routes, bringing tools, precious stones, seeds, and other items from as far away as the Pacific Northwest and the Gulf of Mexico.

ILLINOIS'S PLACE IN THE UNITED STATES TODAY

The city at the center of the Mississippian culture was called Cahokia, located near present-day Collinsville. With as many as twenty thousand people, Cahokia was one of the largest cities in the world between the years 1000 and 1500. Hundreds of smaller farming villages stretching out for about a hundred miles along the Mississippi River surrounded and supported the great city of Cahokia. At the height of its culture, the entire region contained over a hundred thousand people, making it the largest concentration of farming communities in the central United States.

The Cahokia Mounds are ancient hills of earth shaped like flat-topped pyramids built by early Native Americans.

Chapter One

Illinois, "The Real People"

For reasons unknown, the Mississippian culture declined and disappeared. By the seventeenth century, the region was dominated by the tribes of the Illinewek, whose ancestors were the Mississippians. In the Algonquian language spoken by the tribe, "Illinewek" means "the real people" or "the great people." When French explorers first came to the region in 1673, they called the Illinewek the "Illinois."

The twenty-five thousand people who made up the Illinois were divided into smaller tribes called the Cahokia, Kaskaskia, Michigamea, Moingwena, Peoria, and Tamaroa. These tribes inhabited a region that included all of present-day Illinois; parts of Wisconsin, Iowa, and Missouri; and the northeast corner of Arkansas. This region contained a large network of streams, rivers, and lakes.

The Illinois built large permanent settlements along the major rivers in the region, and they traveled the waterways in dugout canoes. To construct such canoes, the Illinois hollowed out large butternut trees by splitting them in half and placing hot coals in the center. The outside of the canoe was then shaped with stone tools.

The trees surrounding Illinois villages were used to make many other items such as spoons, bowls, and canoe paddles. Belts, straps, and bags were woven from thread made from the inner bark of certain trees. Watertight cooking vessels were constructed from bark coated with the sticky gum of spruce trees.

The Illinois also constructed their homes, called longhouses, from forest products. Longhouses were rectangular buildings about 25 feet wide and up to 150 feet long that housed up to seven families each. Each village might have dozens of such buildings.

Longhouses were constructed with logs and covered with elm bark. Inside, the walls were lined with built-in log couches, where families slept together at night using bearskin mattresses and blankets.

Seasonal Schedule

Life in the Illinois village was governed by the cycle of seasons. In spring men hunted small game in the forest and fished the rivers. Women planted crops on the fertile **floodplain** of the river valleys, as their ancestors had done for thousands of years.

The main food source of the Illinois was corn of several varieties including red, white, blue, yellow, and popcorn. The corn was roasted, steamed, eaten as popcorn, and made into soup or a stew called succotash. Women also ground the kernels into flour that was baked into corn bread, johnnycake, hominy, and pudding.

Corn was planted each spring. When the plant was about a foot high, earth was mounded up around the stalks. Beans were planted in these small mounds, their vines climbing up the corn stalks as they grew. Women also planted summer squashes (domesticated from wild gourds), pumpkins, sunflowers, and tobacco.

Besides hunting buffalo and small animals for food, the Illinois people planted such crops as corn to help feed the tribe.

Buffalo hunting could be very dangerous for an Indian brave who had only a bow and arrow.

After the crops were planted, most of the community left the village for five weeks for the summer buffalo hunt. A few women and children stayed behind to tend the crops and to care for the elderly and disabled. A few men stayed to chop wood for the longhouses and protect the village, but most went on the hunt.

Buffalo Bounty

Buffalo were an important resource for the Illinois. The Illinois ate the meat of the buffalo, and they used the rest of the animal to make a wide variety of items. Buffalo skins were used for clothing such as warm winter robes, bags, cooking vessels, and even for the doors of longhouses. The hair of the animal was used for weaving bags and ornaments, for making ropes, and for cushioning beds. Buffalo bones were shaped into arrow points, hoes, and other tools. Organs were used for water bags, string, and musical rattles. Hoofs were turned into glue.

Buffalo lived in the prairie west of the Mississippi River, where they grazed on the tall grasses. Hunting buffalo was a dangerous enterprise even for the most experienced hunters. To capture the huge animals, hunters **stampeded** them into a ring of fire and shot them with bows and arrows. With the help of children, women dried the meat and tanned the hides to take back to the village. When the buffalo hunt was over, the Illinois returned to their villages in canoes loaded down with smoked buffalo meat, bones, and hides.

The Fall Harvest

After the buffalo hunt was over, it was time to begin the fall harvest. The mature corn was stripped from its stalks, dried over a fire, and stored in bark barrels around the longhouse. Autumn was also a time to harvest wild foods such as persimmons, papaws, pond lilies, pecans, and piniki (Indian potatoes). Most of this food was dried and stored in bark-lined pits dug deep into the earth.

When the harvest was over, the tribe separated into small groups for the winter season. Moving from the river plains, they set up camps in the forest. Each family dug a shallow hole in the ground about ten feet in diameter over which they constructed a shelter from logs, hides, and thick woven mats. A firepit for heat and cooking was located in the center of each home.

During cold winter afternoons, men hunted small animals such as rabbits and deer that were easily found by the tracks they left in the snow. During the long nights, families stayed indoors around the fire telling stories.

At the end of the winter season, the Illinois moved back to their longhouses by the rivers. Along the way they stopped to tap maple trees to make delicious maple syrup and maple sugar.

Back in the village, families opened their food storage pits and bark barrels. There, food from the fall harvest was ready to eat. The men hunted and fished while the women planted the next year's crops, and the seasonal cycle began again.

Chapter Two

The Fur Traders

The Illinois people followed the cycles of the seasons for centuries. Their way of life changed dramatically, however, with the arrival of Europeans in the seventeenth century.

By the mid-1600s, English settlers populated America's East Coast. They were followed by French fur traders, who settled in Canada, calling the area New France. The English and French often clashed over control of the fur trade in North America's vast wilderness.

Fur trapping was incredibly profitable, with the furs of deer, otter, bear, marmot, fox, and beaver selling in Europe for 200 times more than they cost in North America. As a result, the lands claimed by France were also coveted by the English. By the middle of the seventeenth century, the French and English were in an ongoing battle over who would rule the fur trade in North America.

Fur-bearing animals were plentiful in North America and drew fur traders from England and France, who sold the furs in Europe for a huge profit.

While these European countries fought over lands inhabited by Native Americans, some tribes aligned themselves with the French. Others sided with the English.

The abundance of fur-bearing animals in the Illinois region attracted the French who came down from the Great Lakes. The fur traders offered guns, knives, iron cooking pots, alcohol, and other European-made goods to Native Americans in exchange for the hides of animals.

Unfortunately the white traders also brought European diseases such as measles and smallpox to which the tribes had little resistance. Great epidemics swept through the tribal populations, sometimes killing more than half of the Native Americans in a given region.

Despite the occasional epidemics, the Illinois worked with the French fur traders. The Iroquois, a powerful group of tribes from the East Coast, hunted animals for the English. When animals grew scarce in the East from overhunting, Iroquois hunters invaded the territories of other tribes in search of more furs.

Around 1650 the Iroquois had forced the Erie and Tionantati tribes to abandon their traditional hunting grounds around the eastern Great Lakes. These tribes moved to Illinois **territory,** where they were welcomed by the natives. Fierce, well-armed Iroquois hunters followed, invading the land of the Illinois tribes. The Illinois had no guns and were easily defeated by the Iroquois, who forced many of them from their traditional homelands.

The Father of All the Waters

The Peoria band of Illinois, driven out of their homeland by the Iroquois, visited a French mission and trading post on Lake Michigan. They described their

Louis Joliet and Jacques Marquette explored the Mississippi and Illinois Rivers by canoe with the help of the Illinois people.

Illinois homeland with its great rivers and fertile river valleys. These descriptions led French-Canadian soldier, explorer, and fur trader Louis Joliet and Jesuit priest Jacques Marquette to explore these bountiful lands. The Frenchmen hoped to claim all the land for the French government, extending New France south from Canada.

In 1673 the band of seven Frenchmen paddled a canoe down the Mississippi River, where they met members of the Illinois tribes. Joliet and Marquette came to the region to map the river, which the Peoria Illinois called "Messipi," meaning "the Father of All the Waters" in Algonquian.

The Illinois were important to the French because they controlled a long stretch of the Mississippi River where the Iroquois had not yet invaded. To the French, the Father of All the Waters was the highway into the heartland of America that they wished to claim for New France. It was also a trading lane to the south end of the Mississippi, connecting to the Gulf of Mexico and the Atlantic Ocean. With control of the river, the French would be able to paddle their fur-laden canoes directly from the midwestern hunting ground to oceangoing ships headed for the profitable markets of Europe.

Friendly Meetings

Marquette had been chosen by the French government to negotiate with the Illinois because he was fluent in the Algonquian language. The Illinois welcomed the French because they wanted help in fighting the Iroquois.

After a friendly meeting, Marquette and Joliet canoed down the Mississippi River all the way to Arkansas. They were forced to stop their journey, however, when they found unfriendly Spanish explorers along the river. On their return trip, the Illinois showed the Frenchmen a shortcut to Lake Michigan on the Illinois River, through the heart of Illinois.

The shortcut took Marquette and Joliet past the large village of another Illinois tribe, the Kaskaskia. The village consisted of 460 longhouses at the great bend of the Illinois River, across from a huge, wind-sculpted cliff, now called Starved Rock near present-day Chicago. Marquette and Joliet promised to return to the Kaskaskia village to build a church, a fort, and a trading post there.

French Visions

The scenic shortcut took the explorers up the Illinois and Des Plaines Rivers and overland to the Chicago River. Here, Marquette and Joliet were the first European explorers to see the land that is now Chicago.

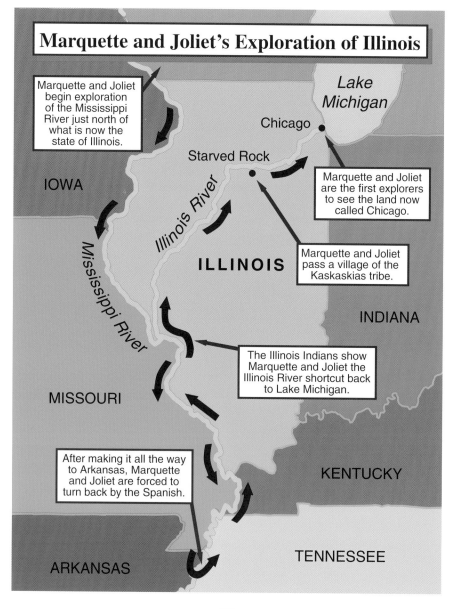

Marquette and Joliet's Exploration of Illinois

Marquette and Joliet begin exploration of the Mississippi River just north of what is now the state of Illinois.

Lake Michigan

Chicago

Starved Rock

IOWA

Illinois River

Marquette and Joliet are the first explorers to see the land now called Chicago.

Mississippi River

ILLINOIS

Marquette and Joliet pass a village of the Kaskaskias tribe.

INDIANA

The Illinois Indians show Marquette and Joliet the Illinois River shortcut back to Lake Michigan.

MISSOURI

After making it all the way to Arkansas, Marquette and Joliet are forced to turn back by the Spanish.

KENTUCKY

TENNESSEE

ARKANSAS

Joliet's map was very detailed in this area, because he foresaw that this site would be key to the development of the whole region. Joliet never returned to Illinois after that first voyage, but Marquette returned to Starved Rock in 1674 to found a religious mission among the Kaskaskia band of Illinois.

Joliet wrote to the French government saying that the Illinois River was the most beautiful place in America to build a settlement. The river was wide and deep and filled with delicious sturgeon and catfish. He saw buffalo, deer, wild turkeys, and swans to feast upon, and open prairies ready for farming. He wrote of forests with huge hardwood trees perfect for making houses and boats.

Following Marquette and Joliet's map, dozens of French priests came to the area to build missions to convert the Native Americans to Catholicism. French soldiers followed, building forts that also served as trading posts for the fur trade. Fur traders soon arrived in the region looking for Native American hunters to work with.

Chapter Three

French Settlers and Indian Battles

At the end of the seventeenth century, the French government created new rules restricting the fur trade. And instead of sending fur traders to Illinois, they sent priests and missionaries to found new settlements in the New World. In 1699 French priests founded a permanent settlement at Cahokia, the ancient center of Illinois culture, near modern-day St. Louis.

The priests came to convert the Native Americans to Christianity, but there were two competing religious orders at Cahokia, the Jesuits and the Seminaries. Both built missions there, and the competition led to a court trial in France. In 1700 Seminary priests were given control of Cahokia, and Jesuit priests moved the Illinois tribes farther south.

Jesuit priests and the Illinois tribes traveled to where the Kaskaskia River meets the Mississippi River and founded modern-day Kaskaskia. The fur trade was still an important source of income for these settlers, and the trading post at Kaskaskia soon became the largest village in the Illinois country.

Other village centers began to form along the fertile floodplain on the east bank of the Mississippi. The land was as productive for the French as it had been for the Native Americans for thousands of years. By the early 1700s, the French had built many small villages along the Mississippi River. Some French farmers and fur traders married Native American women and started families.

Breadbasket of French Louisiana

By 1717, France ruled a large portion of the Mississippi River Valley, including lands in Illinois. The capital of the French territory was hundreds of miles to the south in New Orleans, Louisiana. Farms in Illinois, however, were very important to the survival of New Orleans since the land near the capital region was unsuitable for farming. Instead, corn, beans, wheat, and other crops were grown on the fertile plains of Illinois and shipped south for settlers in New Orleans.

In 1720 the French commander of Illinois country built Fort de Chartres seventeen miles north of Kaskaskia. It became the center of French military control over the entire Northwest Territory.

By 1723 there were 12 white settlers in the village of Cahokia, and 196 in the village of Kaskaskia, the

A Jesuit priest teaches a Native American about Christianity. Most Native Americans fought to keep their own beliefs.

largest settlement. Winepresses and windmills dotted the landscape of the little towns in the area. Apples and other fruits grew in abundance in the orchards.

Using wooden plows, settlers grew mostly corn and wheat on nearby farms. Other crops such as buckwheat, wheat, barley, okra, oats, onions, and tobacco provided variety.

French Farmers

To grow their crops in an efficient manner, farmers cleared long narrow strips of land several hundred feet wide. The land parcels faced the riverbanks where boats could be loaded for shipping crops. The rest of the acreage extended back one or two miles from the shore where the most fertile lands were located. To feed cattle, families shared large community pastures that stretched between several farms.

Farmers lived in houses built from squared logs covered with mud, stones, and straw. Some of these cabins had dirt floors, others had floors made of thick split logs. Steep roofs extended over porches on all four sides of the house protecting the occupants from the sun. Most cabins were surrounded by small gardens, fruit trees, and even vineyards enclosed with fences. Some families used black slaves to help them work the land.

The wild forests and plains surrounding the farms were home to buffalo, deer, bears, and wolves. Most farm families added to their income by trapping animals and selling furs to trading posts in the region.

With a great demand for furs and farm products in New Orleans, a few settlers were able to achieve great wealth. They used their money to buy luxury items imported from France including fine furniture, silver

plates, heavy linens, and candelabras. Some wore clothing made from satin decorated with diamond buttons.

Few French settlers lived like wealthy aristocrats,
however. The average farmer was poor and struggling.
By 1750 there were only about a thousand French or
French-Indian settlers in all of Illinois and about five
hundred West Indian slaves.

Life was hard in the small French settlements
located among little villages of Illinois tribes. Families
had rough handmade clothing and crudely made furniture. Some had no furniture at all, since there were
few skilled craftsmen in the area. Disease, dirty con-
ditions, and the threat of Native American attacks
made the settlements unattractive for most settlers.

*French settlers enjoy a rare celebration. For most, life was
hard in the Illinois region.*

Serious crimes often went unpunished. Land disputes were common since most settlers had no titles to their farms.

Massacre of the Illinois Tribe

While French farmers struggled in the Illinois wilderness, political events in the East were about to change their lives. The long series of battles between the French and English that had begun in 1689 came to an end in 1763, when England defeated the French. England now controlled Illinois, along with almost all of the land from the Atlantic Ocean to the Mississippi River.

The English could not take immediate possession of the lands, however, because they were under attack from a new alliance of Native Americans. Ottawa leader Chief Pontiac had organized several tribes, including the Illinois, to rise up against English rule. The tribes coordinated an attack on English forts and settlements across the region, resulting in the death of about two thousand European settlers over a large area.

In the long run, however, Pontiac's warriors could not defeat the well-supplied English army. By 1766 the chief was forced to sign a peace agreement ending hostilities between the tribes and the English government.

The defeated Pontiac moved onto land belonging to the Illinois, although the tribe members blamed him for their defeat. Pontiac often quarreled bitterly with the local tribes, and in one fight he stabbed an Illinois chief. The victim's relatives were bent on revenge, and an Illinois warrior killed Pontiac with a knife in 1769.

Ottawa chief Pontiac (standing) coordinated several different tribes in attacks against the English.

Seeking revenge for Pontiac's death, the Ottawa, Potawatomi, Chippewa, Kickapoo, Sauk, and Fox tribes united against the Illinois. They attacked the greatly outnumbered Illinois, relentlessly killing all but about 150 of the 3,000 tribe members. The long reign of the Illinois tribes in their native homeland had come to an end.

English Kaskaskia

The few surviving Illinois tribe members moved to the French settlement at Kaskaskia. By this time the English had taken possession of the land and began collecting high rates of taxes on local farmers. Some French people chose to leave the region, selling their possessions and moving south to New Orleans. Others stayed and continued to work the land.

By the 1760s Kaskaskia consisted of sixty-five European families, a few traveling salesmen, and a considerable number of slaves. It had stone houses, a stone church, and a stone house and chapel for the priests who remained leaders of the French settlers. There were also several lawyers in the region who became important leaders while establishing and maintaining French rights in court.

Though the English officially controlled the settlements, the settlers were mostly French and Native American. The English sent a few soldiers and governors but did not attempt to settle in the area. Most of the Illinois were gone, but the dynamics of the territory had changed little during a long, bloody period of Illinois history.

Chapter Four

America's Twenty-First State

Although the English controlled Illinois forts and supply posts, by 1765 the region was of little concern to the British government. In fact, as part of a peace treaty with the Native Americans, King George III of England declared that no land west of the Appalachian Mountains should be settled by British subjects. This meant that Illinois would be preserved as a hunting ground for the Native Americans. George's decree helped the English maintain peaceful relations with the tribes, but it was extremely unpopular with American settlers.

This policy, among others, led Americans to rebel against English rule. In 1775 the Revolutionary War broke out, pitting the American army, led by George Washington, against English soldiers. Almost all of the fighting took place in the thirteen colonies along the East Coast, but there was some fighting in Illinois. At Kaskaskia and other Illinois supply posts, the English traded guns and alcohol to the Native Americans and incited them to attack American settlements.

But the Illinois had been **allies** of the French for a long time, and they never felt at peace under English rule. During the Revolutionary War, most tribes helped the Americans, supplying them with scouts to show **colonial** soldiers the best paths to travel.

The Americans and their allies captured Kaskaskia and Cahokia from the English on July 4, 1778. Meanwhile, tribes loyal to the English attacked the few remaining Illinois villages, killing many women and children while the Illinois warriors were away helping the Americans.

An American Territory

In 1783, after the Americans defeated the British in the Revolutionary War, the new border of the United States was placed at the Mississippi River, which included present-day Illinois. A new set of laws called the Northwest Ordinance created a region called the Northwest Territory, which included Illinois as well as present-day Indiana, Ohio, Michigan, Wisconsin, and part of Minnesota.

General George Washington led the American army during the Revolutionary War.

The ordinance stated that the Northwest Territory would be divided into three to five states when the population of a given area reached sixty thousand. In 1790 the Illinois territorial government was set up in Kaskaskia.

The Northwest Ordinance gave no rights to the surviving members of the Illinois tribes who continued to live in the region. The Illinois aligned themselves with other tribes to fight the Americans but were defeated in 1795. The government forced the natives to sign the Greenville Treaty, which gave the Americans tracts of land at strategic places, including the mouth of the Chicago River, a supply post at Peoria, and another post at the mouth of the Illinois River.

Territorial Changes

In 1800 Illinois had only about twenty-five hundred non–Native American settlers, far short of the number needed to become a state. Instead, Illinois became part of the Indiana Territory. In 1803 the army built Fort Dearborn near present-day Chicago, and about forty white soldiers and seventy white settlers came to live at Fort Dearborn.

By this time members of the Sauk and Fox tribes controlled Native American lands in the territory. In 1804 several chiefs of these tribes were forced to sign away their rights to the land. They sold about 50 million acres of tribal lands in Illinois for $1,000 a year and the right to live and hunt in the area for as long as it was owned by the federal government.

As more and more settlers began to move to the area, the government failed to keep its part of the agreement. Many Native Americans peacefully left, moving across the Mississippi River. This opened the way for the first wave of large-scale settlement in Illinois.

In 1809 the Illinois Territory was created, with its capital at Kaskaskia. The northern boundary of the territory was at Canada, including more than twice the land that now makes up the state. By 1810 about twelve thousand settlers had moved to the Illinois Territory. In 1811 the first steamboat made its way down the Mississippi River, making the area more accessible to settlement.

Fort Dearborn was built in 1803 in the area where the city of Chicago, Illinois, is today.

In 1804 the Sauk and Fox tribes were forced to sign away the rights to their land in the Illinois region.

The Settlers

There were ten times as many Native Americans as whites in Illinois, and they were well-armed by the English in the north. As a result, most white settlement occurred in the southern and central part of the state. Volunteer soldiers patrolled the area, and some local families built large communal forts where they lived together for protection.

Most white settlers in Illinois were poor squatters, who occupied undeveloped land that did not belong to them. The squatters were afraid that if they made improvements on the land, greedy developers would evict them. Finally, in February 1813 a law was enacted that allowed squatters to buy small parcels of the land they had settled. In 1814 when these claims were resolved, the federal government opened a land office in Shawneetown, to sell acreage in Illinois. Settlers poured in from the South and East and laid claim to the wooded land along the rivers.

As settlers streamed into the territory, the natives in the area could see that they were going to be driven from the land. Hoping to maintain peace with the Americans, the Peoria, Kaskaskia, Cahokia, Tamaroa, and Michigamea Illinois signed away their claims to most of southern and central Illinois on September 25, 1818. The lands in northern Illinois, however, continued to be occupied by powerful Native American tribes, such as the Kickapoo, and only the southern third of Illinois contained white settlers.

Statehood

On December 3, 1818, Illinois became the twenty-first state. Although the Northwest Ordinance said a territory must have a population of sixty thousand whites before it could become a state, the region had less than forty thousand white people, the smallest white population of any state in the Union.

Illinois: The Twenty-First State

Lake Michigan

Chicago

ILLINOIS

Fort Dearborn

Peoria

Illinois River

Today, Springfield is the state capital.

Mississippi River

Springfield

Vandalia was the state capital from 1820 to 1837.

Kaskaskia River

Vandalia

Cahokia

Kaskaskia

Ohio River

Kaskaskia was the state capital from 1818 to 1820.

Shawneetown

Kaskaskia became the capital of Illinois. There, **delegates** elected Shadrach Bond the first governor and wrote the first state **constitution**. In 1820 the capital was moved to Vandalia. Seventeen years later, the capital was moved to its present site at Springfield.

Although Illinois did not originally have enough white settlers to qualify it for statehood, today it is one of the most populous states in the Union. A cultural hub at the strategic center of the American heartland, Illinois has often played an important role in human affairs. From the ancient Native American mounds along the Mississippi to the modern skyscrapers of Chicago, the people of Illinois have a long history of reaching for the sky.

Facts About Illinois

State capital: Springfield

State nicknames: Land of Lincoln, Prairie State, Tall State, Sucker State, Corn State

State motto: State Sovereignty—National Union

State song: "Illinois"

State tree: white oak

State animal: white-tailed deer

State bird: cardinal

State flower: native violet

State insect: monarch butterfly

State fish: bluegill

State prairie grass: big bluestem

State fossil: Tully monster

State mineral: fluorite, used to make glass, steel, aluminum

Natural resources: coal, oil, natural gas, lead, zinc, copper, silver, fluorspar, tripoli, barite, lime, clay, sand, peat, timber

Wild plants: wild barley, bloodroot, bluebell, chess, prairie clover, Dutchman's-breeches, lakeside daisy, wild geranium, goldenrod, gumweed, eastern prairie fringed orchid, toothwort, snow trillium, violet

Animals: beaver, coyote, white-tailed deer, fox, white-tailed jackrabbit, mink, muskrat, opossum, river otter, rabbit, raccoon, silvery salamander, skunk, squirrel, turtle

Birds: blackbird, bluejay, cardinal, chickadee, cormorant, crane, crow, duck, bald eagle, snowy egret, falcon, goose, heron, hummingbird, osprey, owl, pheasant, quail, sparrow, wild turkey

Agriculture: corn, soybeans, wheat, barley, oats, hay, apples, peaches, potatoes, pumpkins, turkeys, chickens, eggs, pigs, cows, milk, sheep, lambs, minks

Largest city: Chicago, population about 3 million

Famous people born in Illinois: Jane Addams, Saul Bellow, Edgar Rice Burroughs, Ray Bradbury, Hillary Rodham Clinton, Miles Davis, Walt Disney, Betty Friedan, Black Hawk, Ernest Hemingway, Quincy Jones, Abraham Lincoln, Carl Sandburg

Glossary

allies: People, states, or nations who help one another, especially those who are on the same side in war.

colonial: People or things from the thirteen British colonies that became the original United States of America.

constitution: The system of basic laws and principles that outline the functions and limits of a government.

delegate: An elected or appointed representative of a U.S. territory in the House of Representatives who is entitled to speak but not to vote.

floodplain: The often fertile land next to a river that is subject to flooding.

stampede: To frighten and cause to suddenly run away in panic; especially a herd of animals that moves together.

territory: A subdivision of the United States that is not a state and is administered by an appointed or elected governor and elected legislature.

For Further Exploration

Books

Marlene Targ Brill, *Celebrate the States: Illinois.* New York: Marshall Cavendish, 1997. Traces the changes made to the land and tells about the joys and heartaches of building a community.

Dennis Brindell Fradin, *From Sea to Shining Sea: Illinois.* Chicago: Childrens Press, 1991. Describes the geology, history, economy, and culture of Illinois.

Andrew Santella, *America the Beautiful: Illinois.* New York: Grolier, 1998. Brings to life the geography, history, government, economy, people, and culture that make Illinois unique.

Kathleen Thompson, *Portrait of America: Illinois.* Austin, TX: Steck-Vaughn, 1996. Describes the beauty, splendor, and features that make Illinois a unique part of the United States.

Charles A. Wills, *A Historical Album of Illinois.* Brookfield, CT: Millbrook Press, 1994. An illustrated account of Illinois from the Native American civilization to present-day issues and events.

Websites

The State of Illinois: www.state.il.us. This site features state news, history, and a "Kids Zone" link with information about the environment, nature, and other topics.

Illinois History Resource Page: http://alexia.lis.uiuc.edu/~sorenson/hist.html. Features links to Illinois state symbols and slogans, elected officials, historical topics and maps, women's history, Abraham Lincoln, and related topics.

Index

Picture Credits

About the Authors

P. M. Boekhoff is a professional artist who has cocreated several children's books on the subjects of art and ecology, and illustrated many book covers. In her spare time, she writes poetry and studies herbal medicine.

Stuart A. Kallen is the author of more than 150 nonfiction books for children and young adults. He has written extensively about Native Americans and American history. In addition, Mr. Kallen has written award-winning children's videos and television scripts. In his spare time, Kallen is a singer/songwriter/guitarist in San Diego, California.